Treat Me Easy

Earnest Larsen, C.SS.R.

Liguori Publications
One Liguori Drive
Liguori, Mo. 63057

Imprimi Potest:
Edmund T. Langton, C.SS.R.
Provincial, St. Louis Province
Redemptorist Fathers
April 4, 1975

Imprimatur:
St. Louis, April 7, 1975
+ Charles R. Koester
Vicar General of St. Louis

Library of Congress Catalog Card Number: 75-11322

Photo Credits

Lucie Walsh: pp. 8, 9, 10, 11, 13, 15, 17, 18, 19, 20, 22,
                   24, 26, 28, 29, 31, 33, 34, 36, 37, 39, 41, 43,
                   44, 46, 49, 51, 52, 55, 61, 63, 65, 71, 72, 73,
                   74, 75, 78, 81, 83, 84, 85, 89, 91, 93, 95, 97,
                   98, 99, 100, 101, 102, 107, 109, 117, 118,
                   119, 121.

Earnest Larsen: pp. 56, 58, 64, 68, 69, 78, 87, 104, 106, 110,
                   115, 119.

Layout, art, and cover design: Leona Walsh

Cover Photo: Wallowitch

Table of Contents

Chapter 1

Being able to hear:
I love you.

I love you yes,but
yes,but
yes,but
yes,but
yes,but
yes,but
but

Some words are so big
they're hard to understand.
"Reconciliation" is one of them.
This is tragic;
for now more than ever
is this healing power needed.
Reconciliation
is such a formal-sounding word.
Formal-sounding words often get
separated from the street —
they don't mean much to us.

It's hard to practice something
whose meaning is unfamiliar to us.
But,
if we could translate reconciliation
into a common experience,
it might well suggest the words

"Please, treat me easy."

Who doesn't understand that?
Who doesn't need it?
This is a very nervous time.
People feel frustrated, distrustful, pressured,
powerless, uneasy.
The more nervous the times,
the less inclined we are to reach out,
care,
or offer kindness.
Not many people get treated easy
these days.
There are more than enough people to
complain of a fault,
to make fun of an honest effort,
to criticize a mistake;
there are crowds of people who say,
"Don't be a fool; it can't be done,"
and not many who say,

"Sure you can; give it a try."

So often we want to say,
"I'm sorry,"
when we've misunderstood
someone;
or, "Hey, I really love you,"
when the need just settles on us
like a sunrise.
Sometimes we just need to
throw our arms around someone
who is important to us
or say,
"You really look great."
All those soft, important times
make such a difference
in our lives
when they happen.
But too often they don't get
said or done.
Somehow between the thought
and the act
lies a great chasm
seldom crossed.

Kindness begets kindness;
softness begets softness;
just as
nervousness begets nervousness.
Like ripples from a stone
thrown in a pond,
treating people hard
begets others
treating people hard.

And the street gets so mean.

What are we talking about?
What thought are we trying to nail down?
If we could put it in a word, it would be

reconciliation.

Usually,
we think of reconciliation
in terms of an act to be accomplished.
If we have a fight,
we make up or
"become reconciled" and the problem is over.
That is partially true.
Reconciliation does have to do with the
act of "making up."
But so much more.

Not a half hour ago a young couple came to see me.
Their marriage of seven years was not going well.
They stopped treating each other easy.
They had lost contact with themselves,
and, therefore, with the Word
within each of them.
They stopped listening,
stopped caring.
They both just figured they
knew what the other felt and thought.
No need to talk about it —
besides, the other one wouldn't listen.

Joe
has lost two jobs
in the recent economic squeeze.
This hurt his pride.
He began to doubt
his ability to provide for the family.
Donna went to work.
She was making more than he was.
Feelings about these things
started boiling in each of them —
feelings never faced, never listened to.
Donna had many friends where she worked,
many of them men.
One of them she talked with frequently.
She found she could confide in him;
they could talk about things
she thought
she could never bring up with Joe.
And she told Joe as much.
Joe in his turn,
understanding this as total rejection,
started punishing Donna
in a multitude of little ways.

Mostly with silence.
Why talk?
There was nothing to say;
let her talk to her friend.
(Nervousness begets nervousness.)
The more Joe sulked,
the more Donna played her games.
When they came to me,
Joe said,
"I hope we can make the marriage work because
I love Donna."
He hadn't told her he did in months,
but he felt she "just knew."
Donna
was playing it hard;

*"I'm not sure if I love him or not—
I don't know if I trust him."*

Obviously,
if their marriage is going to make it,
the act of reconciliation has
to take place.
They must both admit they have
been punishing one another,
pledge their good will,
and start opening the doors of
communication.
That is the act.

But that is not enough.
Reconciliation is also a journey,
a process
that must be undertaken.
The act is only a beginning.
The process of continued
reconciliation,
which is at the heart of marriage
and all successful living,
must continue if
they are ever to make it.

Joe must come to admit his own feelings;
he must name the fact that
he fears failure as a provider;
he must admit that he is indeed jealous of
Donna.
He must acknowledge that he has stopped
making her feel as a special human being,
a loved woman.
Then he must reach out.
He must try to understand how Donna feels,
her need to be trusted,
to talk,
to communicate.
Donna must, of course, embark on the
same road.

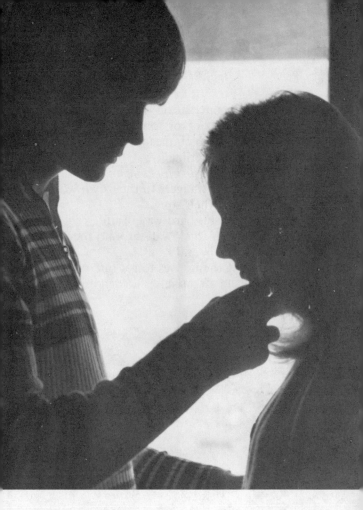

Only if both are willing to live the way of reconciliation
will they ever trust one another.

The word reconciliation is a combination of
re meaning "again" or "anew"
and *conciliare* which means
"to gather in meeting."
Joe and Donna must meet again.
They both are strangers to their own word;
they have lost their song.
To survive in this hard way of life,
they have built thick walls around themselves,
letting no one in and
not allowing themselves to get out.
God has been effectively shielded out as well.

How can we treat anyone easy
until we get used to
meeting ourselves *in the quiet of our own
souls?*
We are such strangers to ourselves.

If this is true with
Joe and Donna,
what about reconciliation on a national level?
How little we listen to or hear one another.

One union at war with another,
farmers fighting with the granaries,
beef producers battling with the public,
oil companies clashing with everyone.
To list them all
would be a waste of time.

Is it any different on a world-wide scale?
Talk to Israel and the Arab nations
about reconciliation,
to the northern and southern Irish.
Talk to India — now that it has acquired the means
to construct nuclear bombs — about all the
peaceful uses of atomic power.

We cannot sit down and talk with reason
because we have lost the sound of our own song;
we cannot treat each other easy because we
no longer know what we are saying.
We do not listen to others
because we do not even hear ourselves.

On the ancient Greek temple at Delphi are the words
"Know thyself" — a reminder that we should
sit in council with our own thoughts and feelings.
By knowing ourselves
we come to understand others:
that they do not threaten us,
that they need not be our enemies,
and that we should extend our hand to them.

If Dr. Kissinger is the prime example of
reconciliation
because he enables others to get together and talk
then perhaps Dr. Karl Menninger is
the psychologist
of reconciliation; for he urges man to go within
and admit to his failings and sin.
Pope John is then perhaps the
apostle of reconciliation.
He had the courage to ask
embarrassing questions:
"What are we, the Church, about?
What are we doing?

Are we fulfilling the law of Christ?"
"Sit down," said Pope John.
"Be in council with yourself,
listen to yourself,
come to know yourself,
and then reach out in brotherly love to
all who would know and see the light."

The continuing process of reconciliation
which is taking place in the Church —
allowing so many more of the brethren to be
treated easy —
springs like a rose on a bush
from the spirit of the great Pope John.

But does opting for reconciliation as a process,
a continuing journey —
rather than just a fact and act —
destroy the concept of security?
How can one be secure
if things are always changing?
"How can I be secure in myself if I am always
open to change?"
How can anything be secure if
change is always a possibility?

Sit in council with thyself.

Not many evenings ago I was privileged to sit by an open lake deep in the woods.

Absent was the noise of traffic,
meaningless conversation — let alone screaming —
trucks, TV, and jackhammers.
There was only silence filled with nature's noises
made by crickets, birds, waves on stones, and
the scamper of chipmunks in the grass behind me.

How deeply we forget that we are nature;
we are born into the cycle of nature;
its song is our song.
But we make up our own songs —
rhapsodies of wealth,
chants of competition,
ballads of fear and isolation —
and then follow them,
wondering where it all went wrong.
As with the crickets and birds
whose security is in the journey,
so ours rests
in knowing we are on the right road.
Security lies not in hanging on to this day,
which surely will pass,
but in the certainty that tomorrow will bring a
new sunrise, a new dawn.

Is not every mile walked computed in
countless steps? And is not each
step a change from the proceeding one?
But how can the mile be covered if we,
foolishly,
remain rooted in this single step — forgetting
it is only in going forward
that the journey is completed?
But we forget —
how tragically often we forget.
Neglecting the healing process of reconciling
with the cycle of nature
that beats within us,
we take root.
We sink our roots in this step,
this second,
this concept,
and forget we are on a journey as
night following day and day
following night.
All thoughts of growth and
passing on beyond where we are at this moment
become lost in the fear of letting go
of this instant now in our grasp.

Old concepts may wear out but
we refuse to let them go.
Old ways of looking and thinking
about what is vital and not vital —
especially in the religious sphere —
may change, *but we will not.*
Door after door opens to us,
offering the rich light beyond,
but we are incapable of passing through them.

Fantastic, powerful, life-giving changes
in psychology, religion, and education
beckon us,
and all too often we say,
"That way threatens my security.
It is different."
We insist on finding security in the moment rather
than the journey.

If we allow no room
for change in our view of
God, self, and others,
then we have indeed boxed ourselves in.

But the security we gain
is the surety of a coffin.
The only growth in cemeteries
is above the ground.
Below — within the coffins —
lies only death.

There is a silly story told about a man
adrift at sea:
All that holds him up is a plank of wood.
For him, the plank spells security.
Along comes a man in a rowboat who will
take him to an ocean liner which will
take him to land
and thus to the completion of his journey.
But the man refuses help.
He will not let go of the plank
in favor of the boat.

At times we are like that man.
In the name of security,
or some other god,
we refuse to admit there might be room for
growth, room for
a more genuine view of ourselves and others,
and a deeper, more Christian understanding
of God.
At such times we deserve the condemnation
uttered against the white man
by the Eskimos of the
frozen North:
"They are so crazy —
they think they are the only ones
who make sense."

The meaning of reconciliation?
A growing ability
to hear and respond to:

Chapter 2

Filtering the word

Hearing and responding with love
sounds so simple.
But is it?
If the process of reconciliation
is not continually happening within us,
are we so sure we actually do hear
and actually do respond to this most important
communication in human life?

The Space Age has taught us
just how deep and total is the
filtration system
surrounding the earth.
We exist in a sack of air.
This covering effectively filters
everything coming to us from outside it.

The light and energy of the sun,
starlight,
cosmic dust —
all are filtered through the layers of air
surrounding us.
Imagine —
no matter how this energy starts out
it is changed in passing through
this filtration system.
We think we know
what the sun looks like,
or the moon.

Yet the various satellites and space probes
show clearly that what we think
we see is not the reality at all.
Actually, the sun is constantly producing
millions of mile-long clouds of energy
and spewing them from its outer layer.
We do not see it that way.
Nor do we, thankfully, feel the effect of
the deadly cosmic rays
constantly piercing our filtration system.
In true science fiction form,
the layers of our atmosphere absorb
these deadly rays before they touch us.
Were it not so,
there would be no life on earth.

So what?

All human beings exist — even as the earth —
within the confines of their own psychological
filtration system.
We are born into and quickly pick up
attitudes, customs, priorities
that surround us like air,
filtering all that comes to us.
Experiences from early life
teach us who we are —
whether we are significant — and
what makes life important.
These too, layer upon layer,
become our filtration system.
Nothing comes to us,
especially the most personal of all messages —
the word of love —
that does not pass through this filter.
There it is changed —
at times totally.

What finally filters through to us
at the core of our protective layers
may well be not what the sender
said at all.
Yet we act and re-act
as if we are certain what the other
meant —
even if that other is God.

The call to
reconciliation —
being easy
with one another —
is the call to look
within and without.
When we know in what way
incoming messages are being filtered,
then — because we truly hear
what is being said —
we have a chance of being easy with others.

There are many people in our culture
who were reared in homes where
affection was seldom shown.
Such was the case with Joe.
He "just knew"
that his parents and family
loved him,
although they seldom, if ever,
expressed it.
Donna's home was different.
Love was not only spoken there;
it was acted out personally.
Joe could not respond in this way.

Those who cannot show affection
live by an unspoken truth:
They must never become vulnerable.
And they are never so vulnerable as
when they attempt to express love
and show affection.

To say, *"I care,"* or, *"I'm sorry,"*
or, *"I love you,"*
opens the door to personal rejection —
a risk many people are not willing to take.
And so, layer-like,
this way of existing surrounds them like a
lead shield.

People who care immensely for them
declare their love;
but, by the time it gets through their
layer of nonvulnerability,
it means something quite different.
They accept love
"as long as it doesn't get too personal."

Being personal demands trust,
And, when trust doesn't happen,
on goes another protective layer.
All too many husbands and wives
do not trust each other.
Not that they fear being lied to
or having their pockets picked.
No, this trust lives on a deeper level —
a level where couples
can share their weakness
as well as their strength;
where they can mutually exchange
their personal feelings, dreams, and fears;
where they can communicate with each other,
confident that what each has to say IS
important and will be accepted as such.

Such trust is not common.
More familiar are couples with
minimal communication and
maximal concealment of the real thing to be said
softly within.
Various groups, built on the premise,
"Whatever you feel, you can say here,"
have made thousands of converts.
Where did this terrible pressure come from,
this immense fear to say,

"I feel....I think....I am...."?

Why do we trust each other so little,
especially husband and wife?
Because, as a result of our training,
we have filtered out love
and replaced it with fear.
So much so
that even if one were to come into our lives —
God-like —
shouting at the top of his heart and lungs,

"You don't have to be afraid.
I love you; I really do,"

he would not be heard.

Like the cosmic rays,
his words would all
be filtered out before
we ever heard them.
I love you, but
I don't trust you;
I love you, but
I won't allow myself to become vulnerable;
I love you, but
I will not allow myself to depend on you.

This fear of dependency is another layer
of the "we don't show affection"
filtration system.
Joe was asked:
"Does Donna
affirm your manhood? Does she
give you certain knowledge that you are special,
not alone, precious for who you are and not just
what you do?"
He said, "She doesn't."
Donna was asked the same question:
"Does Joe affirm your womanhood,
allow you to know that in all this universe
you are special,
you are needed and wanted as a person?"
Donna said, "He doesn't."

They had stopped giving.
Oh they depended on each other
for material necessities,
but they no longer needed each other
as persons.
That for which the marriage existed
had been lost.
Each could get along fine,
or at least just as well,
without the other.
"Never depend."
That is what their filtration systems
said.
They both THOUGHT they knew
what the other was saying,
but didn't.

And then there is God.

Love cannot exist without
trust, vulnerability,
and a special kind of dependence.
And so God's Son says,
*"As the Father has loved me,
so I have loved you.
Live on in my love."*

But, by the time this filters through the system,
our response to what we actually hear may well be:
"I love you too, but I don't trust you enough
to really turn my life over to you,
to really become dependent,
really vulnerable."
Which is not a wholehearted response
to the original message.
And so we have the heartrending spectacle of God
with broken, bloody hands
beating on the protective layers of
our atmosphere —
saying one thing
but having another filter through.

Even to recognize that we,
all of us,
exist within some sort of filtration system
admits of change.
It means we are motivated enough
to name what it is that
alters
the message of love coming to us
from our spouses, children, friends,
and God.
Real security lies in
forging ahead to outer space
rather than doggedly
refusing to admit we live within
our own special atmosphere.
Only by such a process will
authentic reconciliation take place.

Inferiority

Another related but different layer
of our filtration system is
the acquired attitude of some
that they are basically inferior.
This too was built up in early life
and reinforced by multiple, long-forgotten
experiences.
There are countless people who were just
not good enough
for their parents.
No matter what they did,
they were made to feel that
they were not acceptable.
Others were —
perhaps an older brother or sister,
perhaps the boy who could shoot baskets or
the girl who got better grades —
but they were not.
No matter how hard they tried,
their efforts
weren't good enough.
And so they came to believe it.
A thick, suffocating layer seeped over them.

Even though God
shouts into them,

"I love you,"

they continue to respond,

"Yes, I know, but—

I am not good enough to be loved."
And when others tender human love,
they filter it to pity —
answering an authentic offer
with an unyielding refusal.

Twin sisters of these "unlovables"
are those who refuse
to admit their own talents.
When such people
are told,
"You look nice tonight," or,
"That dinner was just super," or,
"You did a great job at the bazaar,"
they invariably say,
"Oh, thank you but not really.
No, not really because
I don't look nice," or,
"The bread didn't rise like I wanted," or,
"Someone else could have done better
at the bazaar."
No matter what they do it isn't good enough,
because they're really not acceptable.

Of course these layers
are invisible,
especially to us.
Only those traveling the road
of reconciliation with themselves
are willing to see and name them.

We are convinced that
what we hear is what is being said;
we are CERTAIN they didn't really mean,
"You look nice."

And the man with a death wish
held fast to the plank
when the rowboat came alongside.

Evidence of another layer
is found in those who proclaim
that they "don't deserve anything better."
Never learning to be good to themselves,
they come to accept that any good thing
is for others — not them.
A trip away from routine,
a prize at a fair,
a truly good friend —
all are things they don't deserve.
If someone were to offer them
pure gold,
they would not take it
because,
they're "not worthy."
And what gold is worth pure love?

Can persons
who exist within this atmosphere
really hear friends and loved ones say,
"I love you"?
Can they hear God?
Oh there can be token acceptance
(the "Yes, yes, I know; that's nice"
routine).
But were someone to deeply ask,
"Why can't you accept that?"
the fight would be on.
The fight of reconciliation.
The test, the challenge to see
whether these persons are willing
to observe and name the layers existing
all around them.
The easy way out,
the "secure" way is to say,
"There are no layers!
There is no such thing as
a filtration system —
at least not around me."

How agonizing for those who love
to confront people
who refuse their love.
(Anyone who feels thoroughly unworthy
cannot accept love.)

But what does God offer us?
What is the Word of God?
What was the message of Christ?
The core of revelation is this:
"We, for our part, love
because he first loved us."
Not because we are perfect —
we never will be;
not because we earned it —
we never can;
not because we are worthy —
for we are not.

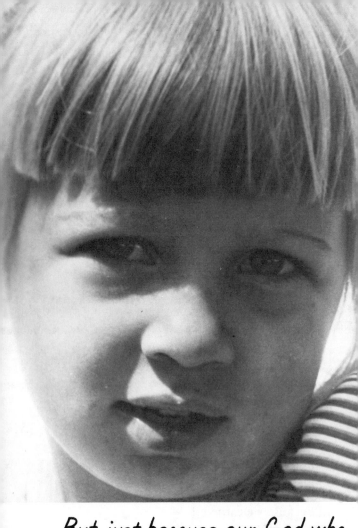

But just because our God who
is a loving Father
DOES.

That's all — he does.
Still, from the fog
of our enveloping atmosphere, we shout,
"I'm sure you do God —
but you can't mean me."

We don't shout this back in words;
that is far too honest.
But it is in our thoughts,
our feelings.
We call it out late at night
when strange ghosts appear
to ask hard questions like,
"It can't be. You don't really think
God loves you, do you?"
And there in the darkness it remains,
unnamed in light,
unfaced in conscious thought,
never brought before the
council table of our mind to be resolved.

We can live legally pure lives
full of religious ritual,
never having faced the core question of Christ:

"Do you accept God's love for you?"

But we can't face that
until we face the problem of our filter.

DUTY

Another layer of our filter system is
duty.
So many in our middle-class, work-ethic
culture are trapped in this
valley of tears.
It goes like this:
We are valued for what we do.
Doing is primary;
getting the job done is more important than
the person doing the job —
so do.
Do till you drop.
Do even if those you do for
don't want or need it.
Do it because doing is good.
Never be good to yourself;
never take a break
because, then, those you do for
won't love you.

So often
people who exist under this cloud
literally work themselves to death —
in the name of love.
And indeed it is love —
but love filtered through a faulty system.

In the name of duty a mother
spends half the night cleaning
"woollies" from the corner,
then does the washing,
then the sewing,
then the scrubbing —
and gets up the next morning,
crabby beyond words.

Love shouts out at her,
"Take it easy.
Everything doesn't have to be done
this second."
But to her it does.
Because loving,
filtered through this atmosphere,
means I am not important —
the job is.

A father works three jobs
to make money for the family vacation,
the extra nice things.
They all tell him to
STOP.
"A thousand times more we'd rather
you be at home
with us
having some fun.
You don't have to kill yourself.
We don't love you because
you provide.
We love you because you are you."
But their message
never makes it.

In the name of love
suicide is committed day after day.

And all the time
mothers, fathers, friends are
CERTAIN
that what they are doing is loving.
There is no reconciliation,
no stopping along the way to look,
to think, and to listen.
Only the most powerful of events could
knock the blinders off heart and eye
to make them see that what
is being heard is not
what is being said.

This attitude toward duty
is often coupled with the thought:
"Hit it hard enough and anything will bend."
People bent on duty are usually
one-line-of-thought people.
Force
comes easy to them.
It is hard for them to
treat others easy.
Their tendency
is to treat people
as problems,
like a sticky valve.
When it doesn't work,
you hit it with a hammer.

It seems they would prefer to ram
a hole in a wall rather
than walk through the door —
in the name of love.

Mere words
fail to describe the desperation
of lovers trying to shout
through the fog to their loved ones:
"**STOP!**
We love you; we want *YOU*
not what you produce.
We don't want your gifts,
your money,
your sweat —
we want you.
Slow down; stop; stay here;
let us talk."

And again, there is God.

To all men the Father speaks
his healing Word,
"Love me, and we will come."
But filtered through this dense atmosphere
comes the response,
"Yes, yes, but first let me finish my
10th rosary; let me finish my 20th prayer.
Let me fast and do penance;
let me first of all . . . . "
And God says **NO!**
"Stop. Right now, just as you are,
now and forever,
I love YOU.
Can you hear that?"
Hesitation —
blinking of eyes, doubt;
then the old familiar response,
"Yes, I know God, but tomorrow I'm
going to join the parish men's club,
visit the sick,
and collect food for starving children."
And God replies:
"Fine — all well and good — BUT
I love you as you are now. Before
all your endeavors.

I love you for who you are, not for what you do.
Can you hear that?
Can you?"

Just recently I had the honor of
working with a man stuck
in his duty system.
He was trying to hear God.
This man was good to the core,
conscientious, active, dedicated.
He said,
"My constant prayer has always been,
'God, I can't. I'm tired. My legs won't go.
Help me. Help me get up and do my duty.'
And God's answer,
as I heard it, was,
'Yes you can! You CAN get up.
You can do your duty!' "
Then, after consciously walking the
road of reconciliation,
of sitting in council with himself,
of listening to himself,
he began to hear a different answer.
"For the first time in my life
I think I really heard God's words
rather than a spin-off of my own
faulty way of hearing.
God now was saying,
'I know. I know you can't.
Let me help you. I never said
you had to do it alone.' "

That man's life has changed —
changed because he named his
filtration system.
Its different layers
had changed the words of love.
And for all of us,
they deeply condition
what we think we hear
as God responds to our prayers.
When you pray,
who answers?

Chapter 3

SUFFERING
The Door of DESPERATION

Who could argue with the judgment
that suffering
is a curse?
Visit a hospital,
see the victims of war,
attend a funeral —
suffering.
Does building up of the kingdom
mean
eliminating unnecessary suffering
from this world of man?

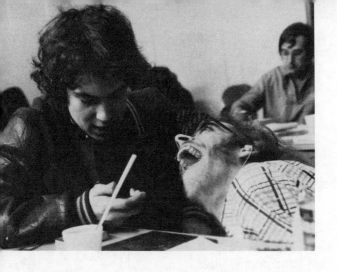

Indeed, yes,
but suffering has a place.
For so often it is the motivation
that impels us
to leave the plank behind,
to take the rowboat,
which takes us to the liner,
which takes us home.
This is what theologians call
redemptive suffering
(which means pain endured
for the sake of salvation).

Others call it
desperation or
hitting the bottom.
But if the goal of Christian life is
to grow,
to progress along the road of Christ,
then whatever is necessary for that journey
is beneficial.

Without the Crucifixion
there could be no Resurrection.
Our crucifixions can lead
to a resurrection,
to an increase of life;
or
they can lead but to further death.
All depends on whether
we learn or not.
The lessons of suffering
are expensive
and compelling.
We do not leave our comfort zone
willingly —
at least not regularly.
Mostly we have to be prodded.
And suffering often supplies this force.

Matt
had never been sick in his life,
which was saying quite a bit.
Only 52, he had
shot every drug there was to shoot,
long before it was fashionable.
He was an alcoholic, a pill popper,
a pusher.
The abuse he dealt his body
was more than anyone should dream of;
yet he never found himself in a hospital.
Two years ago Matt
reached his desperation point;
he hit bottom.
That life was just no good.
He changed
with the help of God and
good friends.

Since then he has not
used drugs,
he has not had
a drink,
and he has been
an invaluable help in
steering others
to this path
of reconciliation.
Then he got sick.

Till that moment, Matt
didn't really believe he could get sick.
His filtration system fooled him;
he thought he was **superman**.
There wasn't anything
he couldn't handle.
God was a good friend but
not one he depended on,
not really.
Of course he never realized this.
If someone were to ask him,
"Do you depend on God?"
he would literally shout back,
"Hell yes; who do you think keeps me
straight?"

Matt underwent open-heart surgery
a few months ago.
Three of the four valves were replaced;
he was given a 20 percent chance to live.
He did.
He is a very tough man.
Then he begged to be released.

Within a ridiculously short time he was
on the street —
healthy in his opinion.
Soon he was back in the hospital with
pleurisy, and much self-disgust.
Why he couldn't even make it a few blocks
without getting tired.
He couldn't run to get out of the rain.
He couldn't work a lick without
getting dizzy.

Again he hit the street;
who was *he* to be sick?
He couldn't be confined to a bed.
A third time he went back to the hospital —
with pleurisy and pneumonia.
Same story.
He couldn't admit he was sick;
he was superman.
Who ever heard of superman being sick?
Desperate now,
Matt finally began to realize
he was killing himself
by not admitting he was sick.
Immensely difficult though it was,
he began to accept his limitations.

Not until this sickness befell him,
this desperation,
would he admit to the truth.
Now he is a much more humble man.
Now he has a very different relationship to God.
Before it was: me and God;
now it is: God and me.
But this light on the truth only happened
through the school of desperation.
More deep lessons are learned in a hospital
than a college could possibly provide.

Louise is a different matter,
but not totally.
Her marriage broke up years ago.
She is lonely, attractive, hurting.
For the countless women in this position,
there are several options open:
to grin and bear it,
to grow old bitterly,
to go the bar routine, or
to become involved in worthwhile activity.
Louise, from childhood on,
has developed the filter system of inferiority.
She thinks she is nothing.
In her mind she is a loser.

Feeling so,
she imagines that
everything she touches turns to dirt.
When her marriage broke up, she took it
in customary fashion:
"I don't blame him.
Who would want to be married to me?"
For now, her option
to overcome aloneness is to hit the bars;
it is a natural.
She knows only too well what waits her there;
she has experienced it often.
More times than she cares to remember
she told herself she has found
"the one."
But "the one" always turned out to be
what she knew he was all the time —
a one-night stander,
a guy who could care less about her.
They come and go.
"What can I do?"
is all that she can say.

How much more will she take?
How great must be her suffering,
her desperation,
before she quits that trail of tears?

If it happens
(please God it does),
she will let go of the plank and
reach out for the rowboat.
At least that.
There are many worthwhile ways to be involved,
ways whose wages are not pain,
ways that would erase
her born-loser image,
ways of reaching out to people
who need and want her.
But for now she will have none of them.

For now,
she is willing to perpetuate her own misery.
She will change —
when her suffering is sufficient to
move her on.

Matt and Louise
may sound like extreme examples
having little to do with us.
But how many of us have suffered enough,
wisely enough,
to be aware of our filtration system?
How many of us have reconciled with ourselves
sufficiently to even admit that
MAYBE
we are not hearing what God is saying?
How many of us are willing to deal
with the basic question of Christ:
"Do you accept my love?"

Minutes ago in the first chapter we
spoke of treating each other easy.
In the last chapter we spoke of treating ourselves
easy.
To turn the corner
requires suffering.
Before we can move to that point,
we must be willing to grow.
But growth calls for suffering.
It is so easy to join the crowd
who put others down and
never seem to tire of casting gloom,
who filter all good things through their
bleak atmosphere, believing nothing good
can happen.
But what does this gain?
Why must it be?

Desperation,
though a terrible thing,
is a door
through which we are pushed.
It was the forced confinement of the
hospital bed
that spelled growth for Matt.
And the misery — when and if it comes —
of unfulfilling relationships
will finally force Louise to come of age.
The pain of a dentist's chair
or a pulled back muscle
can both be teachers
along the way of reconciliation
if only we will listen.

We so often tend to mistake
mere compliance for faith.
Never tested, we readily say
"yes" to almost any dogma of faith.
But the essence of every act of faith
is not compliance but
surrender:
surrender not of our own responsibility
but of our dependence on ourselves;
surrender to the need
not just of a higher Power but a
loving Father;
surrender to the truth that our lives
are but part of a greater Whole —
we are but one cell in the
vast Man
who is Christ.

It is hard to surrender.
We may deceive ourselves
into thinking we have;
then we meet a test only to find
we have not at all.
There are two kinds of surrender —
of the head and of the heart.

The man who finally heard his God say,
"I know you can't — I never asked you to do
it all alone,"
thought he had already surrendered.
But he hadn't.
Not at all.
He was stumbling along trying to carry the
whole load himself — which is exactly
what surrender is not.

How many of the
Christian brethren have truly
surrendered
by allowing themselves to depend
on the Lord?
How many, through the achingly purifying flame
of pain,
have come to admit and name their
limitations, thus
paving the way for their
most authentic act of faith?

"Be at peace" we say to one another.
But the peace which the Lord gives
is the peace that comes from accepting in the heart
that we are not all alone,
that we can depend on God,
that God has called us sons of God.
Have we been there?

Have we gone through that door?

Has desperation taught us the meaning of
true belief?

Only in reconciliation
do we know.

Pain most certainly is not a worthy end
in itself.
It is valuable only in what it causes —
a clarifying of what is.
And once we see things more clearly,
see the many-sided gem of truth
from different angles,
then there is the process —
through reconciliation —
of finding the balance between many things.

Chapter 4
Teeter - totter truth

The danger of
discovering growth through
reconciliation is that
a person might get lopsided.
Insight is a powerful thing;
when we see something for the first time,
we tend to remember it
ONLY from that viewpoint.
In reality, truth is a
many-sided diamond.
To see it is to see it from many sides.
The essential element in the ongoing
quest for truth is that we
name things what they really are.
This is not as easy as it sounds.
For example, at times in trying to decide
which way to turn when faced with a problem,
a person will say,
"I am confused."
Wrong name.
Often it is not confusion by any means;
it is an unwillingness to make a painful decision.

Calling it confusion allows one the out
of not deciding at all.
We cannot deal with a thing if we have
not named it.

Sometimes we say we
hate this or that person.
Hate isn't the word.
Chances are it is a matter of jealousy,
which is actually
insecurity in disguise.
Those who are secure in their own identity
have no need of jealousy.
By calling the feeling
hate or jealousy,
we have put it outside the possibility of
being dealt with —
because that isn't what it is.

In this quest of
reconciliation which allows spiritual growth,
there are some things that simply are
not O.K.,
that are false.
They must be named as such.
Covering up fear of living
by dependency on a mind-altering chemical
simply isn't O.K. — it doesn't work;
accepting the role of
loser
is not O.K., for that is just a
merry-go-round of misery.

Accepting intolerable behavior from anyone,
including yourself,
and calling it good
is not O.K.
That is digging your own grave.

But there are other things not so clear-cut —
not a matter of
being O.K. or not O.K.
but rather a matter of balancing
two truths.
Enter the teeter-totter.

So often truth is much like
a teeter-totter.
When one side is overloaded, it is not a question
of truth or falsity
but rather
one of establishing proper balance
to keep truth sane.

Like water —
we can drown in it or
die of thirst without it.
It doesn't really matter which —
either way we are dead.

Just so with the balancing factors in
reconciliation, like
*honesty, being realistic, sensitivity,
trust in God,
or intelligence.*
Each is true in itself,
each necessary if we are to ever hear God
or anyone else say,
"I love you";
necessary if we are going to ever learn to
be easy with one another.
But —
each needs a balance
or it will crush the bearer.

HONESTY — KINDNESS

In the process of reconciliation we
become aware of the great need for honesty.
There is no argument here —
we must honestly see and name what is,
both in ourselves and others.
But at times we hear people say,
"My big problem is honesty.
I'm just too honest;
it gets people mad and I'm always
in trouble."
Not true.
It is impossible to be too honest;
but it is very possible to be honest without being
kind. *That* causes problems.
There are people who enjoy
honesty for honesty's sake.
It profits nothing.
What is needed is honesty
for the sake of growth,
for the sake of being able to hear all the
"I love you's" coming our way.
And that demands kindness as well as honesty.

Sometimes
we are not ready to hear a truth,
especially a truth said in a cruel manner.
I once heard a so-called
honesty freak tell a girl,
"You'd have all kinds of friends if
you'd lose some of that blubber."
What he said might be true;
but his manner and motive
did not serve for growth in the spirit.
What was accomplished?

"I'm sorry; I've got to call
a spade a spade"
is the creed of some so-called honest people.
But more often than not this means
"In the name of honesty I will punish you."

Kindness
is treating people easy.
It is taking their feelings into
consideration;
it is caring enough to see who they are
before we open our mouths,
and just knowing what they can hear right now
and what they can't.
Kindness is what
tends to make people
accept the truth we have to say,
and, in accepting the truth,
see the light and
hear the Word.

Yet kindness without honesty
is weak and impotent.
More often than not, it is the hiding place
for dishonesty,
false light which can only lead astray.
It is not a question of either/or;
it is both.
One without the other is powerless to
accomplish the goal which is
freedom,
human freedom based on balanced truth.

REALISM — FORGIVENESS

We've all had experience
with realists.
When our brothers and sisters reach out
for something better,
they are the ones who say,
"It can't happen.
Who do you think you are?"
They arbitrarily assert that
Matt will never live without his drugs
and Louise will always be a hooker.
They just can't
see it any other way.
That is their filter system.
But what is realism without
forgiveness?

There are more walking
miracles
on our streets than
can be counted —
reclaimed spirits who once
were down,
dead people who
came back to life.

These persons recovered
not by themselves alone.
Besides the help of a loving Father,
they received, always, the help
of a believing community —
people who see a different scene and
hear a different song.
Not an empty-headed group of dreamers
who refuse
to see things as they are,
but people with hearts big enough to allow for
change, for growth.

I don't know if Joe and Donna will
make their marriage work.
Perhaps as they sit in council together
their
realistic selves will predominate.
All that will
filter through
will be the memory of past injuries,
the fear of similar pain in the future.
If that is all,
they will not make it.
The marriage will die.
If the teeter-totter of truth can
be balanced, however, with the ability
to forgive, it can be saved.

Joe can change.
With help he can see a better way to be
by seeing deeper into himself.
He can admit that Donna needs to be affirmed,
that he has failed in his prime duty as husband.
And the same can be true of Donna.
Realism
sees failure, yes;
but it also foresees healing.

What is true?
Not just reality (admitting past injuries)
or forgiveness (that all must be forgotten).
Both of these are true, and
both are necessary before we can learn
to *treat each other easy.*

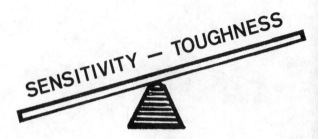

SENSITIVITY — TOUGHNESS

As befits the new mode of being manly,
Andy is sensitive as can be.
He is young.
He writes poems,
thinks he could never be violent,
sings,
feels joy and pain deeply.
He thinks sensitivity is his big problem.
But he is not unlike countless others.
Many
think they can't handle their feelings.
They try to relate to someone
but get hurt;
they try to help someone else and plunge
into worse trouble themselves;
they offer a shoulder to cry on and
end up nearly drowning.
Repeatedly one hears the lament,
"Sensitivity is my big problem;
I just care too much."
No,
it can't be.
It is impossible to care too much,
to be too sensitive.

But it is possible to
be sensitive without being tough.

Again, if water
occasions our death,
what difference does it make
whether we drown or die of thirst?

To be in the process of reconciliation with self
is to be in the process of knowing who we are
and where the balance in our personality lies.
Some don't seem to feel anything,
or very little.
For others every little ripple
sends them into valleys of despair or
onto mountains of transfiguration.
Both types are extremes.

Sensitivity not balanced out by
the discipline of toughness
will kill us.
It clouds up the atmosphere so badly
that no true
"I love you"
can get through.
To allow others to use us
is not a virtue.
The words,
"I'm just a soft touch," or,
"They can talk me into anything,"
often mean,
"See how good I am."
Letting others use us,
destroy us,
shows stupidity.
So many people
mistake a lack of toughness
for sensitivity —
with miserable results for everyone.
"Who helped you the most —
the one who always gave in or
the one who stood up to your con games
showing you the truth?
Who are the people you remember most fondly?"

Reconciliation!
The word, the process
pours through our atmosphere.
What is its message?
Do we hear only what we want to hear or
what is truly being said?

TRUST — RESPONSIBILITY

Strange as it may sound,
some people —
in trying to name their atmosphere —
find that trusting God too much
is their main problem.
It seems they pray and trust
and trust and pray
and don't get what they trustfully pray for.
They just hoped too much in God
who didn't come through for them.
Impossible!
A person cannot trust in God
too much.
It is possible, though,
to trust in God and think that this
removes personal responsibility.
As the song goes,
"Jesus don't pay the rent."
We're not treating people easy
when we convince them
that they need do nothing —
that God will do it all.
God didn't plan it that way.
Ask Jesus.
No one hung on his Cross for him.

"If I pray, why do I still hurt?"
was a spear thrown at me by an angry widow.
Is that the purpose of prayer —
to make all pain go away?
Rather, is it not that by enduring pain
we come to a deeper understanding
of the more abundant meaning of life?

Then there are those whose
problem is they are too smart.
It is just that no one has anything new to say;
they have heard it all.
Every conversation and communication
takes on the air of
teacher to student,
of bored intellectual to struggling novice.
But is it possible to be
too smart? Hardly.
It is very possible for someone to be
smart without being humble, however.
A humble man who is wise
as well as smart always
walks with head bowed.

He is always in a position of respect,
a position of learning.
For even the smallest blade of grass has
much to teach one who will learn.
Is any man so all-encompassing in his
vision
that he knows all there is to know about
everything?
Not long ago I was walking a
Denver street with a young Vietnam veteran.
We passed a derelict sitting on a curb.
The man wore only one shoe.
Some blocks later the veteran said,
"How lucky we are."
"Why?" I asked.
"Because we have two shoes" was his answer.

The wise man always walks with
head bowed —
which is what we ordinarily do
when we pray.
If we are to understand prayer —
which is a form of reconciliation —
we must realize that it too
is a process more than
an act.

Prayer is walking with God.

It gives us an opening to grow,
to hear HIS word filtering down through
the atmosphere of our system.

And the angels
of God
are everywhere
trying, desperately,
to dent our armor.
Only those traveling
with bowed heads
can hear, however.

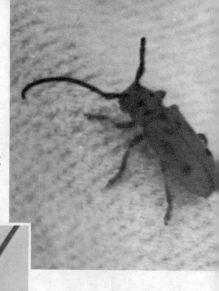

Only they can hear
the crickets speak
of the cycle
of nature,

feel the wind whisper of
God's gentleness,

heed the eyes of a small child
reminding them to treat all things
easy —
easy, for the systems are forming over their heads
and about their hearts.

Chapter 5

Treat Me Easy

Teachers of spiritual growth
stress a most essential and valuable truth:
Our happiness or growth
cannot
depend on other persons.
They cannot tell us
who we are.
Our life is *our* responsibility;
we alone must decide what we will make of it.

These teachers refuse to accept the ruses:
"With the husband/wife I have,
no one could be happy," or,
"You don't understand how terrible life is
at home.
Things just can't get better."
And it shocks them
to hear the worst excuse of all:
"I can't help it —
he/she made my life what it is."

We are responsible for our own lives.
No one can ruin them if we do not yield
that power into their hands;
nor can anyone else make them beautiful.
We do have the power to change what is.
An important psychologist once made this
insightful remark:

*"If you want to know what you really wish
you would have done,
look and see what you actually did.
That
is what you really wanted."*

In this way we place the reward/blame
of our lives where it should be —
on our own shoulders.

But — enter again the teeter-totter,
enter

BALANCE

Most people will agree that their lives
are their responsibility,
but the other side of the coin
demands that we help one another by
treating each brother and sister easy.

There must be a balance between saying,
"That's your problem" and
"Let me give you a hand."

Reaching out to help is a gift.
It *is* our responsibility to place that gift
of concern — that fruit of reconciliation —
at the door of everyone we can.
It is not our duty to open that door, for
we cannot make another's decision for him
no matter how much we would want to.
But if the door of acceptance opens
and we have nothing to offer,
then we are the ones who have failed.

The following teeter-totter truths
should be considered
in establishing a balance between
assuming responsibility for our lives and
treating each other easy.

SEEKING — INVITING

We cannot grow spiritually
unless we seek to do so.
That is our duty.
But it is just as important that someone continually
invite that growth.

The temptation is so strong to
give up,
to give in to jealousy,
to the false need to be perfect,
to the need to be always right,
to the need to play games for attention.
If we think no one cares,
how much more difficult the road becomes!
For those who suffer the filtration system
of inferiority,
how helpful for someone to encourage,
"Sure you can do it,"
"Let's join this discussion club together,"
"Let's bake this cake," or,
"Go out for the team."
There is no guarantee they will make the team
or join the club,
but at least the invitation has been offered.

For those trapped inside the
"I can't show affection" smog,
how important that someone
go in after them.
It is not a matter of indifference
that we put our arms around them,
even though they squirm;
it is not inconsequential that we look them
in the eye and heart saying,

"Hey, I love you."

Invite!

We must invite them to come out,
to abandon their tiny plank
and travel home with us.
To say only,
"Fight it out yourself;
it's your problem; you solve it,"
is not enough.

How tragically many people
walk our streets and ride our buses,
not trusting anyone enough to honestly
relate to them.
They tell no one their pent-up fears,
hostilities, or joys.
Do we ever think to invite them
to speak?
Ask them sometime how the game or day went;
THEN BE QUIET
of tongue and heart
and listen for an answer.
Hear, without taking over the conversation,
what they have to say.
Perhaps not much of importance is said
between husband or wife, child or parent,
because there has been no loving invitation
to speak.

ACCEPTING — FORGIVING

Those who cannot accept or receive
any genuine compliment without a
"Yes, but . . . ." desperately need
someone who gives continuously,

(Like hitting grounders to a small fry —
when you tire of giving him practice
his skill ends.)
We grow spiritually through
repeated acts, acts done over and over.
Those who cannot receive
formed that habit from countless,
long-forgotten acts;
from repeated words that
beat them down and
stole their confidence;
from projects tried and
friendships offered that
failed and were rejected.

They learned they were not good enough to
receive anything precious and lasting.
Who will "hold class" for them long enough
to unlearn that and
relearn something better?

A discerning teacher
crossed paths with a young teen-age girl
who thought she was worth nothing.
Hers was not the ordinary phase of inferiority
most adolescents go through.
This was the real, ugly thing —
a system already solidly formed that
could cause lifelong serious damage.

With patience and care he
sought the girl out,
initiated conversations,
got to know her,
went to her games.
Under the guise of a class project,
he started exchanging a journal with her.
His idea was to get her to ventilate,
to air out the trapped feelings
she cradled within herself.

Months passed.
Hundreds of journal-written words were
exchanged, but nothing real surfaced.
Nothing that truly said,
"I'm hurt," or,
"I'm scared," or,
"I need someone to care about me."
With kind honesty the teacher continued
to give his trust and show his concern.
With respect but not permissiveness
he kept his open hand extended.
As of yet there has been no honest
response —
but the gift is there.
Were the door to swing open,
as soon it might,
it would be there for her to find.
He can't open the door,
but he can place the gift before it.

This is the way of giants!
Refusals abound.
Disappointments accumulate
like slag heaps beside the road.
So many entrapped —
so few offering a way of escape.

"Treat me easy"

is a plea uttered almost everywhere today
if one has but the ears to hear:

*"Don't play my game.
I may seem intolerable,
but don't give up on me.
I know I can't respond
just now,
but, please,
even if I can't ask,
don't refuse to give."*

PATIENCE — ENCOURAGEMENT

People ensnared within the net of
needing to be perfect
have little patience with themselves.
Every little slip,
every slight failure is enough to send them
into the pit of despair.
It takes patience with self
to know one's limits and accept them,
leaving off playing superman or woman.
*Contentedly seeking progress without
secretely coveting perfection is the balance.*
But,
an unwillingness to initially name the trap
and then take the steps necessary once it has
been named means
an unwillingness to be reconciled.

*"True, but help,, me,
treat me easy.*

Mary Beth is a wonderful, beautiful woman —
the mother of five
and the wife of a contented husband.
But she has this problem.
She never does anything good enough
for Mary Beth.
One of her battles is with patience.

Every day she makes a resolution not
to lose patience.
It never lasts.
Sometimes she wonders
whether she should make a resolution at all,
since she seldom keeps it.
But desperately she tries.

Thank God her husband knows;
he just knows what is going on.
He never takes her overseriousness
too seriously.
Even in the middle of an
old tape playing in her head,
"This meal you are cooking —
it won't be good enough;
the cake will crumble, the meat will be too
dry, the potatoes too watery,"
he takes her arm and says,
"Mary,
the meal will be fine.
Even if it is shoe leather,
it will be fine.
(But if it is a shoe
put out the ketchup. O.K.?)"
He can't hang on her cross;
only she can do that.
But his encouragement makes a big difference.

Mary Beth,
for her part, knows her husband
has great difficulty admitting he *needs*.
As long as he is the giver,
things are great.
Admitting dependency
is a real problem for him.
(But spiritual growth demands admitting we are
NOT
the ultimate source of strength.)

Usually with respect and love
she tenderly confronts him in many ways,
especially in their personal life.
Never, on an intimate level,
has he trusted Mary Beth
with his weakness,
his loneliness,
his disappointments.
They are like many married couples.

She often invites,
"How did things go today?
I mean really."
When something obviously is bothering him
she honestly asks,
"What's wrong?"
and is not put off by smoke-screen answers.
Not that she demands he tell her.
(We can't demand loving trust.)
But she does let him know,
"I don't think that is it.
Please tell me —
hey,
you can trust me, you know.
Can you hear me?
I love you."

In such ways do people grow.
In such ways do they invite
the process of reconciliation to proceed.
In such ways do they,
in gentle violence,
knock on the door of the other's inner temple
asking to be let in.

SEEK GOD — CREATE TIME

Conscious contact with God
is a must for spiritual liberation,
which is spiritual growth.
This demands some amount of silence,
a time to be apart,
a time to meet oneself and Creator
at the council table of one's own heart.
We cannot substitute our prayers
for the personal prayers of others;
but we can help someone find
the time and atmosphere
where reflection can take place.

Seek
God—
create
time!

Carol
has people who treat her easy.
She has two children, a sick husband, and
a full-time job.
Her friends are aware of the need for silence.
Silence not just to get away but to get within.

But how can she ever find time?
Regularly, she carves out
three-minute periods of each day to
spend in reflection.
Periodically, more is needed.
And so,
on their own,
these friends just called one night asking,
"Why not let us take the kids this weekend?
you slip on down the coast to the retreat house
and do what you want."
So it happened —
with great profit.

Everyone needs to
"slip away down the coast"
once in a while.
Normally we will not do this of ourselves
unless forced to by sheer desperation.
But, if we would
treat each other easy,
time could be made once in a while.

At a recent convention, the listeners laughed
when I mentioned situations that would be great —
and possible — but just don't happen.
"What," I asked,
"would be your reaction
to this husband-wife conversation?
'I'll take the kids for a few hours.
You just use the quiet to contact your God.' "
They almost fell off their chairs.
It never happens.
Their responses ranged from,
"He would be up to something" to
"I'd think she was nuts."
But why?

If we lament, scream, moan,
and fairly demand that others grow —
that they overcome the problems of their
filtration system —
then why don't we treat others easy enough
so they can do just that?
Creating an atmosphere and time
for prayer is the help they need.

"I can't call your mind's council to order.
But I can quiet the hall
and chase out intruders.
I can build a fire to make the hall warm
and inviting —

the rest is up to you."

At some long-ago meeting
I found this paper.
(Presuming the author's permission —
there was no name on the paper —
I repeat the words here
because they say well
what I want to say.)

The person next to you

Look around you.
  Look around you.
WHO IS THE PERSON — sitting next to you?

The person next to you
  is the greatest miracle and the
    greatest mystery you will ever
    meet at this moment,
  is a testament of the Word made
    Flesh and of God's continuing
    advent into the world — into
    our midst.

The person next to you
  is an inexhaustible reservoir
    of possibility . . .
  with possibilities which have
    been only partially
    touched off.

The person next to you
   is a unique universe of
   experiences, seething with
      necessity,
      dread and desire,
      smiles and frowns,
      laughter and tears,
      fears and hopes —
   all struggling to find expression.

The person next to you is surging
   to become something in particular,
   to arrive at some destination,
   to have a story and a song,
   to be known and to know.

The person next to you
   can live with you, not just
      alongside;
   can live not only for himself
      but also for you;
   can comfort, encounter, understand
      you, if that is what
      you want —
   and, in turn, he is to be
      understood also.

The person next to you
   can never be fully understood;
   is more than any description
      or explanation;
   can never be fully controlled,
      nor should he be.

The person next to you
   believes in something,
      something precious;
   stands for something,
   counts for something,
   lives for something,
   labors for something,
   waits for something,
   runs for something,
   runs from something,
   runs toward something.

The person next to you
   has problems and fears,
    wonders how he is doing — and often
      doesn't feel very good about it,
   is often undecided and disorganized,
    and painfully close to chaos —
   but endowed with great toughness
    in the face of adversity, able
    to survive the most unbelievable
    difficulties and persecutions.

The person next to you
   is a whole colony of persons —
    persons met all during his
    lifetime;
   is really a community in which still
    live a father and mother,
    a friend and enemy.

The person next to you
  has some things he can do well,
  some things he can do better than
    anyone else in the whole world;
  there is something his one life on
    earth means and cares for —
  but does he dare speak of it to you?

The person next to you
  is Mystery, and the
  WORD MADE FLESH IS MYSTERY.

    " . . . and the WORD WAS MADE FLESH
    and dwelt among us . . . . "

  So, brothers and sisters,
    Look around you —

For He is Here!